GRAND

STATE STREET TO EAST STREET, 1830-1970

WALK
NEW HAVEN
CULTURAL HERITAGE TOURS

A PROJECT OF THE Ethnic Heritage Center

Use this QR code to access
this tour with a hand-held device

The Ethnic Heritage Center
270 Fitch Street, New Haven, CT 06515
Phone: (203) 392-6126
www.ethnicheritagecenter.org
E-mail: info@ethnicheritagecenter.org

ISBN: 979-8-7662678-9-8

To purchase copies of this and other Walk New Haven tour books, visit walknewhaven.org.

COVER Pre-1945 Topo Map of New Haven 1890. Courtesy of the University of Texas Libraries, The University of Texas at Austin.

Contents

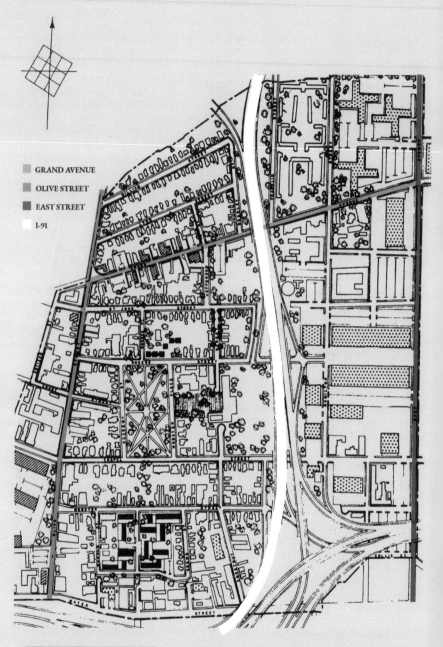

GRAND AVENUE
OLIVE STREET
EAST STREET
I-91

Illustrative Site Plan for Wooster Square Renewal Plan, 1965, showing the segregation of the residential and industrial areas created by Interstate 91 and Urban Renewal.

Introduction

This *Walk New Haven: Cultural Heritage Tours* guide is the fourth volume in a series created by the Ethnic Heritage Center (EHC). Although some of the buildings described are no longer standing, their stories remain. This self-guided walking/biking/driving tour tells the pre-1970 stories of the experiences, contributions, and hardships faced in New Haven by several of the diverse cultural and ethnic groups that have enriched our community.

A major goal of the EHC is to stimulate interest among the many additional cultural groups in New Haven to form historical societies to preserve and share their histories. This book is part of that process. We plan future volumes and have created a project website (walknewhaven.org) where we will continue to post additional information on existing tour sites, as well as adding new sites important to our community's many cultural groups.

The EHC was founded in 1988 and currently has five member historical societies, which have selected the sites to include on our tours:

- Jewish Historical Society of Greater New Haven, founded in 1976
- Italian-American Historical Society of CT, founded in 1979
- Connecticut Ukrainian-American Historical Society, founded in 1983
- Connecticut Irish-American Historical Society, founded in 1988
- Greater New Haven African American Historical Society, founded in 2003

The EHC has been located on the campus of Southern Connecticut State University since 1992, where the archives of most of the societies are preserved.

This book has been funded through matching grants from the Community Foundation of Greater New Haven and the Jewish Foundation and Jewish Federation of Greater New Haven as well as by many generous donors to the Ethnic Heritage Center.

The Ethnic Heritage Center encourages the public to follow us on Facebook and Instagram and to share information about our tour sites, additional sites, and any inaccuracies. You may contact the EHC at 270 Fitch Street, New Haven CT 06515, info@ethnicheritagecenter.org.

.

Cultural History of the Inner Grand Avenue Neighborhood

State Street to East Street, 1830–1970

For the purposes of this tour, we refer to the area centered around Grand Avenue between State and East Streets as "Inner Grand Avenue" to emphasize its proximity to downtown and to distinguish it from other segments of the same road in Fair Haven and Fair Haven Heights. While other names are possible for this distinctive sub-neighborhood, we felt it was important to use a term that asserts the centrality of Grand Avenue as a defining feature of the corridor, while making clear that the area is historically and culturally different from other parts of Grand Avenue because of its closeness to downtown and the geographical barrier of the Mill River.

The post-1850 evolution of Inner Grand Avenue (between State and East Streets) exemplifies one of the overarching themes of all Walk New Haven tours:

Aerial maps illustrating impact of urban renewal and I-91 construction. By 1965, part of the harbor had been filled in for I95 and Route 34 had replaced the Oak Street /Legion Avenue neighborhood.

the adaptation of commercial, religious, and social spaces to accommodate cultural and demographic change. Select any address on the avenue, look it up in city directories from different eras, and you will find vivid traces of social transformation: a vaudeville theater becoming a Pentecostal church for Latin American immigrants, a kosher butcher shop becoming a nonprofit social services agency, a bank becoming a dry goods store and then a furniture warehouse, or a similar shift in use as new immigrant groups populate the neighborhood, bringing with them different economic and social needs. Sometimes this process of evolution and accommodation has coincided with sudden, massive changes in the built environment, such as urban renewal; more often it has occurred incrementally, and less disruptively, within the existing urban footprint. Even the manner and scale of transformation have thus evolved, according to the political appetites of each era; in the dynamic churn of the city, the only constant is change.

What became Grand Avenue was a thoroughfare as early as the 1600s. It evolved into a significant road in the 1800s with the completion of the Barnesville bridge (1819) over the Mill River and the development of Fair Haven as a suburb of New Haven (later annexed to the city in the 1870s). After New Haven's incorporation in 1784, this portion of Grand Avenue closest to downtown was part of a mixed residential-commercial area called "New Township" that lay east of the original Nine Squares and included the area around Wooster Square.

The southern part of the New Township began to develop in the 1810s and 1820s; the northern part, around Grand Avenue, in the 1830s and 1840s. New Haven's first railroad, the New Haven & Hartford, was completed along the neighborhood's eastern edge, just past East Street, in 1839. The line ended at New Haven's Belle Dock, where a steamship line transported passengers to South Street in Manhattan in a five-and-a-half-hour trip.

Two early communities of free Blacks developed in the area. One, in the triangular notch created by the intersection of Grand Avenue and State Street (part of which was colloquially known as "Negro Lane"), was displaced in the 1840s by the building of the New Haven & New London Railroad. The other community, to the south and east along the banks of the Mill River, was known as "New Liberia," a reference to both the West African settlement created by the American Colonization Society for emancipated slaves, and to the Liberian Hotel owned by local African-American entrepreneur William

Lanson, who lived in the neighborhood himself until financial troubles and legal persecution landed him in the almshouse.

Early industry included rope-making facilities (known as "rope walks") and warehouses that served the maritime economy around New Haven Harbor. Also located in the area were slaughterhouses, stables, and a bell foundry. (An 1824 map by well-known cartographer and silversmith Amos Doolittle actually refers to Grand Avenue as "Bell Lane.") In the late 1800s Grand Avenue became an important streetcar route, with the maintenance facilities and power plant for the Connecticut Trolley Company located at the midpoint of the avenue. Manufacturing and heavy industry developed in the area because of its proximity to both Long Wharf and the steamboat wharf (in an era when coal and other raw materials were typically brought in by ship), easy access to trolley lines and to downtown. The 1865 city directory noted: "Today no thoroughfare into the city is more thronged than Grand."

The inner part of Grand Avenue has had long ties to the Jewish community, including some of the earliest Jewish settlers in New Haven. Of Sephardic

State and Grand, 1915

descent, Jacob Pinto was one of New Haven's first recorded Jews, immigrating around 1758 with his brother Solomon. Jacob prospered and built one of New Haven's first brick houses at the prominent intersection of Grand and State. A half century later, German Jewish immigrants settled the blocks of Grand Avenue closest to downtown. The Heller and Mandelbaum Dry Goods Store was established by German Jews at 5 Grand Street (changed to Grand Avenue after the Civil War). It established a precedent for Jewish retail business on the avenue, though its primary significance was as one of the earliest meeting places for Congregation Mishkan Israel, Connecticut's oldest synagogue community.

1938 Grand Avenue Business Men's Association newspaper

The Inner Grand Avenue corridor developed as a working-class and immigrant community centered around the presence of major industrial employers (including hardware, carriage, clock, rubber, corset, and paper box factories) and the avenue's bustling commercial strip, which offered goods and services of all kinds—from groceries, candy stores, and specialty butcher shops to shoe, clothing, and hat stores. In the twentieth century, Grand Avenue west of Jefferson Street became a destination sought out by shoppers for its furniture and home goods retailers, many of them Jewish-owned, such as Kruger's, Unger's, and Marcus'. Some of New Haven's best-known and longest-running family businesses occupied dense storefront blocks along Grand Avenue (Lucibello's, Horowitz Brothers, DelMonico), before moving away as they became more successful and expanded, or as the avenue's fortunes declined. Few local businesses survived the impacts of urban renewal; Lucibello's was a rare exception that remained and thrived.

Venues for recreation and entertainment created spaces where diverse ethnic and religious communities could inter-mingle. When the Boys Club (founded in the 1870s) moved to Jefferson Street in the early 1900s, its basketball court and swimming pool helped to create lifelong memories for youth of all backgrounds. Local theaters like the Dreamland and the San Carlino were cosmopolitan spaces where different ethnic groups encountered one another in the enjoyment of vaudeville, cinema, and other entertainment. Lillian's Paradise was a popular restaurant and jazz club founded by an Alabama-born female entrepreneur who sought opportunity in New Haven as part of the Great Migration of African-Americans from south to north in the early twentieth century; hailed for both the quality of its food and its musical offerings, the club was patronized by African-Americans and whites alike. Famed Italian-American opera diva Rosa Ponselle got her start performing on Grand Avenue, as did Jewish clarinetist and jazz legend Artie Shaw (*né* Arshawsky), whose uncle owned a local butcher shop. Like so many other immigrant neighborhoods, Inner Grand Avenue was a musical place that captured the city's broad cultural mosaic.

Religious institutions were a social and cultural, as well as spiritual, anchor for many local immigrants. For six decades Congregation Mogen David capably served the "Grand Avenue Jews" — even non-members would go there to help make a *minyan*. St. Patrick's Church was founded in the 1850s by Irish Catholics and became a fixture in the neighborhood for religious services and

education. Among those who settled in the area and worshiped there were John Madigan, an 18-year-old who emigrated as soon as his apprenticeship as a harness maker was completed; James Reynolds, activist for Irish independence, who opened a foundry in the neighborhood; and Thomas Cahill, son of Irish immigrants, mason and ornamental plasterer, and colonel of the 9th Regiment Connecticut Volunteers (the state's "Irish Regiment") in the American Civil War. St. Patrick's Church continuously served the local Catholic community for more than a century until closing in the 1960s.

Just as St. Patrick's was a spiritual anchor, the dominant economic anchor for the Inner Grand Avenue neighborhood throughout much of the 1800s and 1900s was the New Haven Clock Company. In the period 1850-1920 it became one of the largest clockmakers in the world — occupying 28 buildings — and the neighborhood's largest employer, with as many as 2000 workers turning out close to 500,000 timepieces every year. Its presence in the neighborhood drew immigrants from all over the world and supported a wide range of local businesses centered around the commercial strip of Grand Avenue.

Grand and Franklin with Dreamland Theatre, 1927

In the heyday of the clock factory, workers and their families lived in tenement-style housing on the avenue as well as small one- and two-family houses on side streets. As the area's nineteenth century housing stock deteriorated and economic privation increased during the Great Depression, the Farnam Courts public housing project was developed by the City's new Housing Authority at a location along Grand Avenue near Hamilton Street. Opening to great fanfare in 1942, the racially mixed Farnam complex offered 240 units of new housing for working families and was the third public housing development in New Haven, after Elm Haven in Dixwell and Quinnipiac Terrace in Fair Haven. The neighborhood was thriving as both public and private sectors successfully functioned to meet the community's social and economic needs.

Dreamland Theatre, c. 1950s

In the 1950s and 1960s, two cataclysmic events led to the decline of Inner Grand Avenue as a vibrant zone of mixed residential and commercial use: the demise of the clock company in 1956, presaging a decades-long wave of de-industrialization and disinvestment; and the construction of Interstate 91, beginning in the early 1960s, which separated Farnam Courts and St. Patrick's Church from downtown and the bustling commercial section of Grand Avenue. The interstate required substantial use of eminent domain and directly or indirectly led to the bulldozing of anchor institutions like Congregation Mogen David and St. Patrick's Church. Meanwhile the New Haven Redevelopment Agency's Wooster Square Project called for "clearance" (demolition) of "slums," substituting in boxy modern buildings made of concrete, and surface parking lots. Although urban renewal unfolded differently in Wooster Square than in other parts of the city, and the southern part of the neighborhood around Wooster Square Park was spared large-scale disruption in favor of "rehabilitation," the northern half of the neighborhood, around Grand Avenue, was less fortunate and lost the majority of its historic buildings, its walkability, and human scale.

With de-industrialization and urban renewal, many residents and businesses moved to the suburbs. Population began a long decline. The area west of the highway remained largely residential, while much of its retail commerce shifted to the suburban malls and shopping centers. The area east of the highway became dominated by industrial and wholesale commercial uses, with a smattering of retail businesses like Ferraro's meat market and grocer. The old clock factory buildings were subdivided and, thanks to cheap rents and easy access to the highway, enjoyed a raucous second life as a venue for nightlife and adult entertainment of all kinds.

The first decades of the twenty-first century have brought more changes, including signs of rebirth. Beginning in 2012, the Farnam Courts project was demolished and rebuilt as Mill River Crossing. In 2013 the City of New Haven released a new development plan for the "Mill River District" (between I-91 and the river, on both sides of Grand) in an effort to bring precision manufacturing, light industry, and other job growth to the area. Then in 2018, the City approved a plan to remediate the polluted clock factory complex and redevelop it as artist lofts. As it has for centuries, the area continues to evolve in complex and unexpected ways.

Grand Avenue Site Map

This map shows two types of sites on Grand Avenue, between State and East Streets: standing buildings (blue circle) and demolished buildings (gray squares). For standing buildings, this map key indicates if the historic use is a current or a former one. These and additional historic sites in the area may be found on our website at walknewhaven.org.

1 5 GRAND | **First Congregation Mishkan Israel, Heller & Mandelbaum Dry Goods** *(demolished)*

2 GRAND AND ARTIZAN | **Rafael Melendez Corner**

3 ARTIZAN (BETWEEN COURT & GRAND) | **Artizan Street School** *(demolished)*

4 950 GRAND | **DelMonico Hatter** *(demolished)*

5 935 GRAND | **Lucibello's Pastry Shop**

6 915 GRAND | **Unger's Flooring**

7 907 GRAND | **Kruger's Furniture and Appliance** *(demolished)*

8 765 GRAND | **Perelmutter's Department Store** *(demolished)*

9 879-81 GRAND | **The Terese Furniture Company** *(demolished)*

10 857 GRAND | **San Carlino Theater** *(former)*

11 830 GRAND | **Orchowsky Butcher Shop** *(former)*

12 GRAND AND JEFFERSON | **Lenzi Park**

13 31 JEFFERSON | **The Boys Club** *(former)*

14 16 BRADLEY | **Congregation Mogen David (Bradley Street Shul)** *(demolished)*

15 751 GRAND | **Miller's Clothes** *(demolished)*

16 785 GRAND | **J.F. Shanley Dry Goods** *(former)*

17 724 GRAND | **Lender's Bagel Factory** *(former)*

18 624 GRAND | **St. Patrick's Church** *(demolished)*

19 GRAND (BETWEEN I-91 & WALLACE) | **Farnam Courts** *(former)*

20 686 GRAND | **Rosner's Grocery Store** *(demolished)*

21 664 GRAND | **Ferraro's Market** *(former)*

22 635 GRAND | **Sisk Brothers Funeral Home** *(demolished)*

23 654-6 GRAND | **Marzullo's Bakery** *(former)*

24 137-9 WALLACE | **Lillian's Paradise** *(demolished)*

25 133 HAMILTON | **New Haven Clock Company** *(former, partially demolished)*

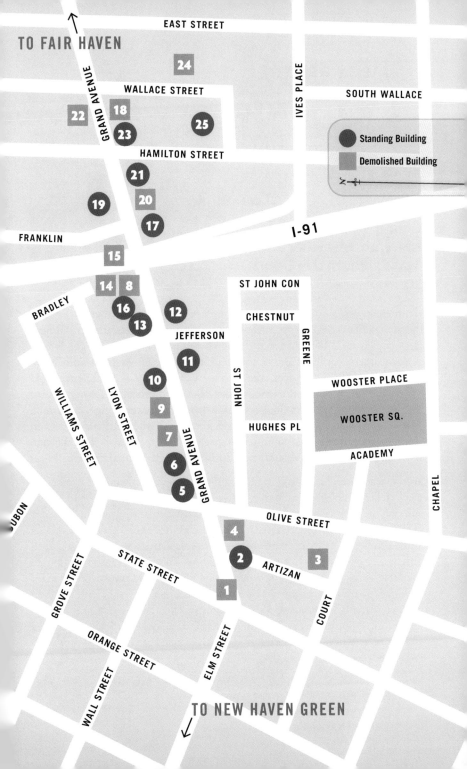

JACOB HELLER,
Wholesale and Retail dealer in

CLOTHING,
AT UNION HALL,
No. 138 Chapel Street, New Haven, Conn.

1

5 GRAND STREET—EARLY NAME
FOR GRAND AVENUE

Congregation Mishkan Israel, above Heller and Mandelbaum Dry Goods Store (demolished)

Jacob Heller and Louis Mandelbaum were first cousins who arrived together in the United States in 1837 from the town of Dennenlohe, Bavaria, in southern Germany. Around 1840 they started a family business — a small dry goods store at the northeast corner of Grand and State Street. The Heller and Mandelbaum store (located at 5 Grand Street, according to city directories — it was not changed to "avenue" until 1887) was a modest operation, and probably less well known than the building's second floor occupant. It was above the dry goods store in 1840 that Congregation Mishkan Israel, the first Jewish religious society in Connecticut and the oldest continuous synagogue congregation in New England, was established. Michael Milander was the society's first spiritual leader.

Several years later, Heller and Mandelbaum each pursued their own businesses, with Heller establishing a clothing store on Chapel Street and Mandelbaum entering the grocery business. Congregation Mishkan Israel continued to meet at 5 Grand until moving to larger rented space in the former Brewster Building at the southeast corner of State and Chapel Streets. In 1856, the congregation purchased a building on Court Street, the former Third Congregational Church (pictured here). The synagogue remained on Court Street until 1897, when it relocated to its first purpose-built sanctuary at the corner of Orange and Audubon streets (currently the home of the Educational Center for the Arts magnet high school). In 1960, a larger synagogue and religious school building was designed and constructed on Ridge Road in Hamden, where the congregation remains today, 180 years after its founding.

Congregation Mishkan Israel synagogue building 1856-1897 (former Court Street meeting house of the Third Congregational Church).

2

GRAND AND ARTIZAN
Rafael Melendez Corner

Rafael A. Melendez Sr. was an outstanding leader of New Haven's Puerto Rican community, breaking barriers in public service and building a network of civic institutions to serve his community. Relocating to Connecticut from Coamo, Puerto Rico, in 1953, he moved to New Haven in 1955 to work as a machine operator at Winchester Repeating Arms Company (following in the footsteps of Gumercindo Del Rio, another pioneer in the Puerto Rican community, who already worked at the gun manufacturer). After leaving Winchester, Melendez embarked on a career of public service. Melendez was one of the first Latinos to pass the civil service exam and become an officer in the New Haven Police Department. Later he became the first Latino foreman at the city's Department of Public Works, where he worked for more than 32 years until his retirement in 1998.

As a leader in New Haven's Puerto Rican community, which doubled in size between 1960 and 1980, Melendez was instrumental in starting Junta for Progressive Action in 1969 along with Gumercindo Del Rio, Pura Delgado, Marcos Ocasio, and Carlos Rodriguez. Junta was the first multi-service agency for the Latinx community in New Haven. Melendez also served as vice president of the Puerto Rican Civic League, vice president of the Spanish-American Club, and as a founding member of the first Hispanic Baseball League.

The corner of Grand Avenue and Artizan Street, near his longtime home at Friendship Houses co-op, was named for him in 2012. Melendez died in 2015.

Rafael Melendez

3

Artizan Street School *(demolished)*

The Artizan (or Artisan) Street School near the corner of Artizan and Court streets was one of several segregated New Haven grammar schools for African-Americans in the mid-1800s, including one on Carlisle Street in the Trowbridge Square area (then known as Spireworth) and another on Goffe Street. Each school was typically led by an African-American woman — such as Sally (sometimes called Sarah) Wilson or Elizabeth Price — giving instruction in her home to students of various ages. (There were no "graded" schools at all in New Haven until 1853.) The classes were often overcrowded — according to school records, in 1861 Wilson had only 93 spaces available in her makeshift "classroom" but taught 120 students, tutoring them in shifts because of the limited space. African-American teachers like Wilson and Price were paid only $200 a year by the school district when the average annual salary at that time for all teachers was $390; for female teachers, $293, and for male principals $1,500.

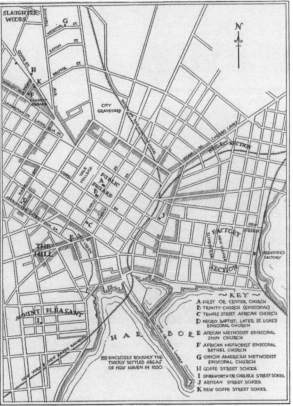

The New Haven Board of Education passed a resolution in August 1863 declaring that "African or colored children" should receive the same resources from the school district as other children. The same year the Board agreed to support the Goffe Street Special School — the first purpose-built school for African-American children in New Haven (see Walk New Haven's Lower Dixwell tour) — which subsequently absorbed much of the enrollment from the Artizan Street School.

After the Civil War, legally sanctioned school segregation in Connecticut was abolished by state statute (1868). Wilson does not appear in school records after 1866. There are no known photographs of her.

The best-known graduate of Wilson's school was Dr. Edward Bouchet, who is believed to be the first African-American to earn a PhD (Physics, 1876) from an American university and one of the first known African-American graduates of Yale University.

LEFT PAGE *1861 New Haven Public School Records mentioning Artizan School and Sarah Wilson*
ABOVE LEFT *Photo of Dr. Edward Bouchet from 1874 Yale College Graduation*
ABOVE RIGHT *Reference Map for Early Negro New Haven 1810-1850*

4

950 GRAND AVENUE

DelMonico Hatter

(demolished)

Established in 1908 by Ernest DelMonico as "Del Monico The Hatter," the venerable New Haven headwear store was originally located on the ground floor of 950 Grand Avenue, near the corner of Olive Street. Ernest's son Joseph DelMonico ran the store for seven decades, from the 1920s until his death in 2001 at age 90. Joseph's son Ernest DelMonico II ran the store from 2001 until his death in 2018, reinventing it as an e-commerce retailer that ships worldwide from its storefront location on Elm Street. The store had previously moved to State Street in the early 1960s, then to a location on Elm Street in 1965, and to its current location at 47 Elm in 1982. Delmonico won a "Hat Retailer of the Year" award from the National Headwear Association in 2008. In the 1940s there were 27 hat stores in New Haven (including another one on Grand Avenue owned by Isidore Ladin, father of Jewish Historical Society of Greater New Haven founder Harvey Ladin), but DelMonico is the only one that remains. It is currently run by fourth-generation family member Ben DelMonico.

Del Monico The Hatter, 950 Grand Avenue c. 1918.

5

935 GRAND AVENUE

Lucibello's Pastry Shop

Francisco Ciccio, the bakery's founder, was born in Amalfi, Italy, in 1897. He excelled in school through the eighth grade before becoming an apprentice for his two uncles in a department store. In 1908, a powerful earthquake in Sicily and southern Italy nearly destroyed the city of Messina and killed much of the area's population, including Ciccio's uncles. Ciccio arrived in New York in 1920 with little money before moving to live with family in New Haven. He went back to New York for employment opportunities and there discovered his love for baking. After becoming an American citizen and marrying Filomena Proto, he changed his name to Frank Lucibello, a surname taken from other members of his extended New Haven family.

He traveled and learned different techniques before starting his own business in New Haven: Lucibello's French-Italian Pastry Shop on Chapel Street, which opened in 1929. Specializing in French as well as Italian pastries and cakes, Lucibello's soon became very popular. Andrew Faggio was a close childhood friend of Lucibello and asked Lucibello to give a job at the bakery to his ten-year-old son. Andrew's son Frank Faggio started working at Lucibello's and continued there until he purchased the bakery from Lucibello in 1959. When urban renewal arrived a few years later, Lucibello's was forced to relocate to its present location at the corner of Grand Avenue and Olive Street, where it continues to operate under the management of Frank Faggio's son Peter. Today many of the bakery's patrons are second-, third-, even fourth-generation customers who come from all over the region to pick up Lucibello's delicious cakes and pastries.

TOP LEFT *Chapel Street interior 1959 with Frank Faggio* TOP RIGHT *935 Grand Avenue* BOTTOM LEFT *474 Chapel location*

TIES THAT BIND

Arnold Unger, center, is flanked by his two sons, Robert and Philip. Unger's Floor Covering celebrates 50 years.

Unger's has kept in step with market

By Miguel Almeida
Register Staff

NEW HAVEN — At Unger's Floor Covering in downtown New Haven, plaques and certificates on showroom walls laud the company's distinguished work for the past 50 years as a supplier of carpets, vinyl and

and we've come through in great shape."

Unger's sprouted in 1946 in a small storefront on Congress Avenue. Arnold Unger, having returned from World War II after serving in the Army and Merchant saw an opportunity as home booming in the years following

"We believe the customer is always right," he said.

"Floor covering is something that people buy once or twice in a lifetime, so we make

UNGER'S FLOOR COVERING

6

915 GRAND AVENUE

Unger's Flooring

Arnold Unger was born in the Bronx in 1917 and moved to West Haven, Connecticut as a child. His parents were Jewish immigrants from Hungary and Austria. He had an initial career managing night clubs in the New Haven area, including Jake's on Savin Rock. By chance, he entered the flooring business after returning from overseas service in World War II, finding a job at New Haven Tile on Congress Avenue across from College Plaza. When the owner left, Unger took over the business in 1946 and also opened a smaller Unger's Cut-Rate store on Goffe Street. In 1965 he consolidated the two stores as Unger's Flooring on Grand Avenue near East Street. In 1980 he moved closer to downtown at the current location on Grand Avenue between Olive and Jefferson. He continued working until he passed away in 1999 at the age of 81. Arnold's son Bobby took over the business and continues to operate it today. Bobby attributes the store's longevity to its good reputation for quality service. The year 2021 marks the 75th year of Unger's doing business in New Haven.

TOP *1967 newspaper story* BOTTOM *Unger's Floor Covering, 2021*

7

907 GRAND AVENUE

Kruger's Furniture and Appliance *(demolished)*

Kruger's Furniture and Appliance was one of many family-owned furniture stores on Grand Avenue in the late 19th and early 20th centuries. Kruger's sold many household items, such as chairs, lamps and couches. Anti-semitism sometimes made it difficult for Eastern European Jewish immigrants to get work in the local factories, so instead they opened businesses to provide goods and services to the factory workers. The building was demolished in the late 1960s. Today, 907 Grand Avenue is a parking lot adjacent to Unger's Floor Covering.

Kruger's Furniture and Appliance c. 1960

8

Perelmutter's Department Store *(demolished)*

Perelmutter's Department Store, at 735 Grand Avenue, was another local business started by a Jewish immigrant. Benjamin Perelmutter was born in 1883 in Rovno, Ukraine. His father died when he was nine years old and at fourteen-and-a-half, Benjamin was already the general manager of a store in Rovno. He emigrated to Canada at 21 to live with his brother before marrying Bessie Horowitz (also from Ukraine) and moving to New Haven, where Bessie's aunt lived. Once in New Haven, Perelmutter worked as a peddler, traveling around Connecticut selling clothes, dry goods, and yard goods to people's homes. After two years, he saved enough money to open a storefront. The couple worked alongside each other for 16-17 hours per day, selling men's and women's clothes. The business did well, and Benjamin was able to purchase other buildings for his business. The couple spoke Polish and Russian, so some of their customers were of Polish and Russian descent, but customers represented the diversity of the neighborhood. Bessie organized fashion shows for the neighborhood after the business expanded to selling baby clothes, women's hats, and wedding dresses. Bessie passed away in 1968 and Benjamin continued the business until 1969, when he sold it to Michael Rachlis, one of his employees, and continued working with him. After a fire broke out in the store, Rachlis moved the business to 63 Boston Post Road in Orange. The Perelmutters were members of B'nai Jacob Synagogue and are buried in the B'nai Jacob Cemetery in New Haven.

Perelmutter's Department Store c. 1960

THE NEW HAVEN REGISTER, TUESDAY, APRIL 2, 1963

the **TERESE FURNITURE CO.**
879 GRAND AVE.
GOING OUT OF **BUSINESS**

Mrs. Terese Falcigno, owner and manager of THE TERESE FURNITURE CO. is retiring from the retail furniture business after 44 years. Mrs. Falcigno was associated with the P. J. Kelly Furniture company for 18 years and for the past 26 years has been in business on Grand Avenue. The building which houses THE TERESE FURNITURE CO. is part of the Wooster Square Redevelopment Project, and is scheduled to be demolished.

SAMPLE BARGAINS	BARGAINS IN OUR GIFT DEPARTMENT	SAMPLE BARGAINS
7 Pc. Kitch. Sets Coppertone 69.50	Wall Figurines	Hide-a-bed 139.50
Utility Tables 4.50	Wall Plaques	Cedar Chests .... 19.50 Up
Detecto Hampers 5.00	Candy Dishes	3 Pc. Maple Bedroom Set .. 89.50
3 Pc. Livingroom Sets 139.50	Clocks	Box Spring & Innerspring
Upholstered Hi-Chairs Maple 12.50	Floral Pieces	Mattress 49.00
Set Mahogany Dining	Maple Wall Accessories	2 Pc. Early American
Chairs (6) 50.00	Maple Wall Racks	Livingroom Set 149.50
5 Pc. Maple Dinette Sets .. 49.50	Corning Warr	Lawson Sofa Bed 62.50
Boston Rockers 19.95	Figurines	Desk & Chair 25.00
Plate Glass Mirrors ... 5.00 Up	Maple Group Pic	Maple Hutch — Sample .. 48.50
Cricket Chairs 6.50	Religious Figur	
Maple Cellarette 59.50	Many items in our Gift De	
Occasional Tables ..... 2.00 Up	are imported from Germany	
Table Lamps .... 1.00 to 17.50		
Floor Lamps 5.00		
Bridge Lamps 4.00		
Glass Door Bookcase 21.50		

Everything in the store must be sold.
thru-out our four floors. Visit our Ba

"I promise the people of New Haven big savings on fine
FURNITURE CO. has carried in stock for the past 26 years."

SALE STARTS WEDNESDAY

the **TERESE FURN**
879 GRAND AVE. Phone 624-2878 OPEN D

9
879-881 GRAND AVENUE

The Terese Furniture Company *(demolished)*

In 1919 Teresa DelPreto Falcigno went to work for P.J. Kelly, owner of some of the city's most successful furniture stores, at his Grand Avenue location. When Mr. Kelly died in 1921, Teresa partnered with his son Edward to continue to operate the Grand Avenue store in the same building where P.J. had started. When the Kelly family sold the business in 1937, Edward and Teresa became partners in their own store at 879-881 Grand Avenue. In the 1940s Edward sold his share of the business to Teresa, who renamed it The Terese Furniture Company. It became one of the largest female-owned business in New Haven. It had four floors and sold complete furniture sets, appliances, and carpeting, and included a high-end gift shop. Teresa was a labor force of one, acting as salesperson and bookkeeper, with home deliveries provided by Teresa's husband and family members. The store closed in 1963 amidst urban renewal and the building was demolished. Its original location is now partially occupied by the modern building at 795 Grand, which has been a karate studio, storefront church, and currently (in 2021) Kiddie Korner Daycare.

LEFT *Teresa DelPreto Falcigno 1940* CENTER *The Terese Furniture Co. 1957* RIGHT *1963* New Haven Register *ad.*

10

853-857 GRAND AVENUE

San Carlino Theater *(former)*

Opened in 1909, the San Carlino seated over 500 patrons and had a full orchestra pit for live musical performances. It was owned and operated by Richard T. Halliwell, who also owned smaller theaters in Meriden and Ansonia, offering vaudeville and other low-cost entertainment to working-class, often immigrant audiences. An unusual feature was the all-female house orchestra.

The San Carlino was ill-suited to the new era of "talking movies" and disappeared after 1927. Another theater, the Apollo, occupied the site until the 1940s when it was replaced by the Dreamland Theatre a block away as Grand Avenue's major entertainment venue. The distinctive three-story building that housed the San Carlino has survived and is now occupied by a church (Manantial De Vida).

Italian-American operatic soprano Rosa Ponselle (1897-1981), *née* Rosa Ponzillo in Meriden, gave some of her first performances at the San Carlino around 1914, when she was still a teenager. She recalled having to rehearse and perform two sets of songs: one in English for "Yale boys" who trekked a mile from campus, and another set of traditional Neapolitan songs for Italian-speaking immigrant "townies." James Ceriani, Italian-born proprietor of New Haven's popular downtown club Café Mellone, discovered Ponselle at the San Carlino and brought her to the attention of famous Italian tenor Enrico Caruso; by age 21 she was performing on the stage of the Metropolitan Opera in New York. Ponselle went on to a long and distinguished international career, but always remembered the San Carlino fondly in interviews late in her life.

San Carlino Theater c. 1915.

11

830 GRAND AVENUE

Orchowsky Butcher Shop *(former)*

Born in Russia in 1878, Jewish immigrant Isaac Orchowsky operated a butcher shop and kosher meat market at 830 Grand Avenue. He lived above the store with his wife and four children, all of whom worked in the store. An empty lot next door (now Lenzi Park) was used for slaughtering chickens. Orchowsky's was one of several kosher butchers operating in the Inner Grand Avenue neighborhood in the early 1900s, including Bailey's and Epstein's. Kosher butcher shops not only fulfilled a religious obligation for observant Jews, but also served as a kind of communal "watering hole" where religious and nonreligious Jews alike could *kibitz* and exchange information. In the early 1930s Orchowsky moved his market farther out Grand Avenue to Fair Haven. He died in 1940.

Isaac Orchowsky's nephew was the acclaimed jazz clarinetist Artie Shaw (1915-2009), who grew up nearby and assisted his uncle in the meat market as a youth, practicing his C-melody saxophone in the back of the shop. (Only later did he switch to clarinet.) Artie dropped out of New Haven High School at 15 and left New Haven to become a touring musician. After becoming world-famous for his big-band recordings of tunes like Cole Porter's "Begin the Beguine," the clarinetist wrote about growing up in the Inner Grand Avenue neighborhood, and his early artistic influences in New Haven, in his acclaimed 1952 autobiography *The Trouble With Cinderella: A Study of Identity.*

After the departure of the Orchowsky Meat Company, 830 Grand housed a tie store and then a furniture and upholstery company. It is currently used by Project MORE, a social service agency.

LEFT *830 Grand Avenue in 2021* RIGHT *Artie Shaw* LOWER RIGHT *Artie Shaw and Billie Holiday*

12

GRAND AND JEFFERSON

Lenzi Park

The lot on the east side of Jefferson Street between Grand and St. John was a chicken market in the early 20th century, run by Arcangelo Pacelli, who immigrated to New Haven in 1898 at age 13 from San Salvatore Telesino in southern Italy. Selling poultry and eggs, the market served a multi-ethnic clientele. At times a rabbi would come and slaughter chickens according to kosher laws for the local Jewish community. Pacelli had four children who all worked in the store. He moved the market to Liberty Street in the Hill neighborhood before retiring. He died in 1979 at age 94.

During the urban renewal period, the site was abandoned and became a blighted lot. Acquired by the City of New Haven in the 1970s, it was developed into a city park with open space and a play area (later removed) designed by renowned landscape architect Dan Kiley. The park was named after a local Italian-American war hero, Private Joseph W. Lenzi (1922-1945), who was born across the street in 1922. Lenzi was killed in action on the Pacific Island of Iwo Jima during World War II and awarded the Silver Star posthumously for gallantry in action. Relatives of Lenzi still live in the area. The mural at the north end of the park was completed by a youth group affiliated with Catholic Charities of New Haven. The park is currently maintained by a neighborhood group, Friends of Lenzi Park.

Private Joseph W. Lenzi, Lenzi Park 2021

13

31 JEFFERSON STREET

The Boys Club *(former)*

The Boys Club of New Haven was founded in 1871 by philanthropist Eliza Maria Blake (wife of inventor Eli Whitney Blake) in her home across the street from the New Haven Green, at a time when city leaders began to recognize that the growing immigrant population needed recreational facilities as well as social services. It was only the third Boys Club in the country. (Today there are more than 4,600.) In 1891, the club moved to 200 Orange Street, a hub for social service organizations known as the United Workers building (which was demolished in the 1920s to build the Hall of Records). The club remained at that location until 1915, when it moved into a new facility on Jefferson Street, half a block from Grand Avenue. This location was closer to the factory workers' families whose children were served by the club.

During its six decades on Jefferson Street, the club was the only recreational facility in the neighborhood, a welcoming place where boys could play sports as well as games like ping pong, checkers, and table hockey. The Boys Club contained a gym with a basketball court, which provided fun and exercise even in the depths of winter. Talented hoopsters went on to play in state and even national competitions. The club's swimming pool was the only public pool in the area; generations of local boys learned to swim there. *(Continued on next page.)*

1938 photo of United Workers Boy's Club

The club offered camaraderie, mentoring, and a lifetime of memories. Locals who grew up playing there recall the excitement of receiving free sneakers when the club was chosen to serve as a testing site for U.S. Royal, an athletic shoe manufacturer in Naugatuck. Others recall the stern but well-meaning truancy officer who lived in the building and ensured that youth were not skipping school to play games or loiter at the candy store on Grand Avenue.

The Boys Club of New Haven was one of the first in the nation to welcome young women, becoming the Boys and Girls Club in 1970. The club moved to a new facility on the corner of Sargent Drive and Hallock Avenue in the early 1970s. The new facility was named the Albie Booth Memorial Boys and Girls Club, in honor of the New Haven native who became a star football player at Yale during the years 1929-31 and died tragically of a heart attack in 1959. In 1989, the Club moved to 253 Columbus Avenue in the Hill neighborhood.

After the Boys Club relocated, a new youth services organization opened at 31 Jefferson in 1992: Leadership, Education, Athletics in Partnership (LEAP), which serves underprivileged children in the area. LEAP continues the work of the Boys Club into the 21st century.

1909 photo of boys at pool table

14

16 BRADLEY STREET

Congregation Mogen David *(demolished)*

From 1903 to 1966, Congregation Mogen David (also spelled Mogin David) was the center of Orthodox Jewish life for the "Grand Ave Jews." As the neighborhood's Jewish population surged with the arrival of Eastern European Jews in the early 1900s, the small synagogue was often packed during special occasions. The building had two floors, with a first floor and gallery for the men and the top floor for women. The basement was a social hall used for *kiddush* (food and drink after a service), special gatherings, and a space for children during the holidays. Harold Miller, whose grandfather's clothing store was located around the corner, remembers his grandfather being called to help make a *minyan* of ten required for the recitation of certain prayers, even though he belonged to a different synagogue.

Congregation Mogen David was attended by most of the Jewish merchants along Grand Avenue and their families. The men were typically well-educated in religious traditions and were able to read the Torah and even conduct services. When prominent rabbis would visit and speak at the synagogue, donations would be raised to present them with honoraria.

During the urban renewal period, the synagogue's property was needed for Interstate 91 and, along with the nearby Miller's Clothes, was sold to the State of Connecticut. The subsequent demolition of Congregation Mogen David was the end of an era for the "Grand Avenue Jews."

Congregation Mogen David, 1957.

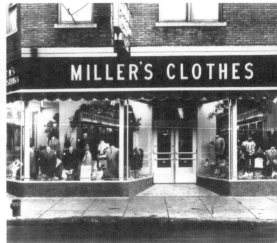

15

751 GRAND AVENUE

Miller's Clothes (demolished)

Isadore (Izzy) Miller, born in a small town on the Poland-Russia border, arrived in New Haven in 1908 by way of New York. He came to start a new life, joining relatives who had settled in New Haven a few years earlier. He married Elsie Marcus in 1914 on the third floor of Elsie's sister's house in the Wooster Square area. He was 20 years old and she was 17. Within three weeks Izzy opened a tailor shop off Grand Avenue which eventually became Miller's Clothes, a full-service men's and boys' clothing store at 751 Grand.

Isadore and his brother Joe were skilled tailors, and customers from many backgrounds came from all over the city to buy tailored suits from the store. The business was a staple for the men in the area because, as Miller relatives later recalled, "no one left there empty-handed."

Outside of his business, Isadore Miller was a scholar of Jewish texts and a founder of Congregation Keser Israel on Foote Street, where he served as a cantor. Because his store was just steps from Congregation Mogen David on Bradley Street, he would often be called on to join worshippers there to help make a *minyan* (at that time, ten men) for daily services.

Miller's Clothes remained on Grand Avenue until 1961, when the State of Connecticut acquired the property for construction of Interstate 91. Two stores across the street, Perelmutter's Clothing and State Candy and Tobacco, remained. Isadore joined his son Mack at Mack Miller's clothing store on Whalley Avenue.

Miller's Clothes in the 1950s

16

785 GRAND AVENUE

J. F. Shanley Dry Goods *(former)*

The adjoining Romanesque Revival-style buildings at 779-785 Grand Avenue were built around 1900 by John F. Shanley. Born in New Haven in 1861, Shanley was the son of Irish immigrants. His father worked as a manual laborer. John grew up on Franklin Street and started his own business on Grand Avenue as a dry goods merchant and "gents furnisher." He was also an agent for European steamship lines, which allowed relatives here to arrange passage for relatives "back home" in Europe. These brick buildings were the location of his store for many years.

Shanley was a member of several fraternal benefit societies, including the Ancient Order of Hibernians. He became active in New Haven politics as a director of the Free Public Library, a member of the Board of Finance, and a two-term alderman. He also served three terms from 1905 to 1911 as a Democratic State Senator from the 11th District.

785 Grand Avenue in 2021, John F. Shanley c. 1905

17

724 GRAND AVENUE

Lender's Bagels *(former)*

Harry Lender was born in Siedliszcze in eastern Poland in 1894. He learned to bake as a baker's apprentice in Lublin, Poland, where he met and married his wife Rose and started his family. When anti-Semitism made life dangerous, he followed his older brothers to New York in 1926. He worked for a bagel shop in New Jersey until 1927, when he bought a small shop (about 800 square feet) on New Haven's Oak Street, which he named The New York Bagel Company since he made New York-style bagels. He then sent for his wife, two sons, and daughter. In 1935, Lender bought a two-family house with a 1,200-square-foot garage, the former home of the Regna Italian Bread Bakery, on nearby Baldwin Street in the Hill. His sons Hymie, Sam, and Murray helped him there for 30 years, introducing modern production methods such as freezing the product, using a large rotary oven, and baking many varieties of bagels. As the business grew, Harry and Rose continued to be known for their generosity and always maintained the practice of supplying free bagels to community events and people in need.

When Harry died in 1960, his sons Marvin, the operations manager, and Murray, the marketing manager, took over the business. As they expanded their clientele to include supermarkets across the country, they needed more modern production space and bought a 12,000-square-foot facility in West Haven in 1965, which they expanded into 25,000 square feet, naming it the Lender's Bagel Bakery. Needing still more production space, in 1975 they bought an even larger facility at 724 Grand Avenue in New Haven that formerly housed the Olmer Brothers Bakery. By 1984, the Lenders had four bagel factories producing more than 750 million bagels a year. In 1984 they sold the business to Kraft. According to Marvin, "There were four or five companies, including Sara Lee, that wanted to buy us. There was a bidding war." Marvin and Murray continued working in their respective roles for two more years before retiring and devoting their time and financial resources to many philanthropic projects which have benefited both the Jewish and non-Jewish community. Lyman Orchards acquired the property in December 2021 with plans to relocate their fruit pie-baking operations to New Haven.

LEFT *Lender's Bagels plant after production was halted* RIGHT *Murray and Adam Lender in the Grand Avenue bakery.*

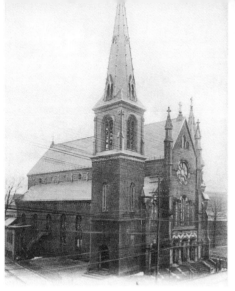

18

624 GRAND AVENUE

St. Patrick's Church *(demolished)*

By 1850, the influx of new Irish immigrants to New Haven amid the "Great Hunger" back in Ireland led to the designation of a second Catholic parish in the city. (The first had been Christ Church, built in 1834 where Yale New Haven Hospital is currently located. It was destroyed by fire in 1848, renamed St. Mary's and reopened in 1848 on Church Street until 1874 when it relocated to its current location on Hillhouse Avenue.) In 1851 the cornerstone for St. Patrick's Church was laid on the southwest corner of Grand and Wallace, soon to be followed by a parish school on Hamilton Street, staffed by the Sisters of Mercy. The original church, destroyed by fire in 1875, was rebuilt at the same site in 1876.

In 1868, in a highly unusual arrangement between the New Haven Board of Education and the Church, the parish school became a public school and was renamed Hamilton Street School. The Sisters of Mercy continued to comprise the majority of the teaching staff. For more than 100 years, St. Patrick's Church and Hamilton Street School were at the core of neighborhood life, serving generations of immigrants and their children. The school was closed in 1959 after a fire and the church was demolished in 1966 during the period of urban renewal and construction of Interstate 91.

LEFT *St. Patrick's Church before hurricane of 1938* RIGHT *Interior and post-1938 photo*

19

GRAND AVENUE BETWEEN I-91 AND WALLACE STREET

Farnam Courts *(demolished, rebuilt as Mill River Crossing)*

The origin of Farnam Courts can be traced to the Wagner-Steagall National Housing Act of 1937 which created a system of federal subsidies for local housing authorities and ushered in the first wave of public housing in the United States. With the support of New Deal-era Mayor John Murphy, a Democrat elected in 1931, who championed housing reform and infrastructure projects that would provide construction jobs, the Housing Authority of New Haven was formed in 1938 and seeded with $5.5 million from the federal government. Farnam Courts was the Housing Authority's third development, after the 487-unit Elm Haven complex in Dixwell (completed in 1941) and the 318-unit Quinnipiac Terrace in Fair Haven (completed in 1942).

Designed by versatile local architects Douglass Orr and R.W. Foote, Farnam Courts was completed in 1942 with 300 units spread across 7.7 acres. It was named after Yale economist and philanthropist Henry Walcott Farnam (1853-1933), who was the son of prominent New Haven railroad tycoon Henry Farnam. With its patios, courtyards, and ample play areas, Farnam Courts was primarily geared toward young families. In contrast to the older cold-water tenements in the area, some of which were so crowded they were referred to disparagingly as "beehives," the new affordable apartments at Farnam offered modern conveniences, reliable heat, hot water, indoor plumbing, and playgrounds. There was also a community hall and on-site health clinic.

On paper Farnam was racially integrated: the majority of residents were white but approximately one-third were African-American. Farnam renters worked in local industries such as the clock, rubber, and hardware factories, the English Station power plant, or small businesses along Grand Avenue. The complex offered residents a village-like atmosphere with its own newspaper and sports teams.

By the 1960s, the decline of the clock factory and other local industry, combined with urban renewal and the construction of Interstate 91 just steps from residents' homes, destabilized the neighborhood and left Farnam Courts both physically isolated and, increasingly, racially segregated. Exposure to pollution from the interstate highway, English Station, and other environmental hazards left residents suffering from some of the highest rates of asthma and respiratory illness in the state. Meanwhile, deferred maintenance mounted as local budgets tightened and the federal government withdrew political and financial support for public housing.

Beginning in 2012, the original buildings were demolished in a $30 million redevelopment of the site by the Housing Authority (now Elm City Communities) that also resulted in the renaming of the complex, now known as Mill River Crossing.

LEFT *Neighborhood housing on the site in 1940 before demolition for the construction of Farnam Courts* ABOVE *Farnam Courts opens in 1942*

20

686 GRAND AVENUE

Rosner's Grocery Store *(demolished)*

Rosner's Grocery store was a popular neighborhood establishment started in the 1930s by Eli Rosner, a Jewish immigrant from Austria who eventually owned and operated eight grocery stores across the New Haven area. All the stores served the ethnically diverse working-class community that developed around area factories. Rosner's was known for allowing customers to shop on credit, as did many other businesses in the neighborhood during the lean years of the Great Depression. Customers would write out the list of items they wanted to buy, as well as the price and the date they got the items. On the following Friday, when workers got their paychecks, Rosner's customers would pay for their purchases. Alphonse Proto, in his memoir *It Was Grand!*, recalls that Rosner's grocery store had open barrels of pickles and olives so that customers could reach in and help themselves to snacks. Eli's grandson Scott Rosner remembers that when Sally's Apizza was just starting, Eli would let the now-famous Wooster Street pizzeria take whatever supplies it needed and pay whenever the restaurant's revenues improved. In the early 1950s, Eli branched out to start Grocer's Wholesale on the west side of New Haven. Eli passed away in 1962 at age 61; his two sons, Russell and Eddie, operated the store until it closed in the mid-1980s. The Grand Avenue property was acquired and demolished by the New Haven Redevelopment Agency in the 1960s.

TOP *Rosner's Food Market c. 1950s* BOTTOM *Eli and Sarah Rosner with son Russell 1932*

21

664 GRAND AVENUE

Ferraro's Market *(former)*

Joan and Salvatore Ferraro Sr. opened Ferraro's Market in 1973. Salvatore was born in 1928 in Bristol, Connecticut, to parents who had emigrated from Naples in southern Italy. He used his training in the meat business to become a co-owner of the Mohawk Market on State Street in 1952. When the New Haven Redevelopment Agency acquired and cleared the Grand Avenue site as part of urban renewal, the Ferraro family opened a "one-stop neighborhood market" on Grand, directly across from Farnam Courts where there was more foot traffic. In 2020, Ferraro's had 100 employees, half of them family members. Sal and Joan's four sons, Sal Jr. (who died in 2010), John, Peter and Mark, started working there when young. Peter ran the business side, with John and Mark "on the [meat] saw." The third generation worked alongside them. Sal Jr.'s daughter Victoria learned all aspects of the business, having worked at the store since age 14. She began using social media to promote Wednesday specials for seniors and students. Prepared foods were very popular and were cooked onsite by cousin Jason and Chef Giuseppe from Italy. On December 24, 2020, amidst the Covid-19 pandemic, Ferraro's closed the Grand Avenue store. Orlando and Fernando Cepeda from Brooklyn, New York opened The Meat King Farms at the Grand Avenue site less than a week later.

On April 28, 2021, Ferraro's opened a new market on Universal Drive in North Haven.

TOP *Ferraro's Market, 1973* BOTTOM *Salvatore Ferraro Sr. and son Salvatore Jr. in the Meat Room*

22

635 GRAND AVENUE

Sisk Brothers Funeral Home *(demolished)*

Now located in Hamden, Sisk Brothers Funeral Home was originally located at 635 Grand Avenue.

Founders Edward, Patrick, John, and Thomas Sisk were the sons of Irish immigrant Patrick Sisk, who came to New Haven in the late 1850s. For most of his life Patrick listed himself as a "carman," also known as a "cart-man," a common profession among Irish immigrants. Cart-men drove horse-drawn carts for hire that were the primary method for local collection and delivery of goods. As urbanization made walking funerals less practical, cart-men were employed to collect and transport the deceased, giving rise to the occupation of undertaker and the funeral home industry. In the 1870s Patrick listed his occupation as undertaker at the same address as his residence. Patrick died at age 49 in 1879 and his sons continued the business. Sisk Brothers moved from Grand Avenue to Dwight Street in the early 1930s, and the Dillon Brothers Casket Co. purchased the building.

Sisk Brothers funeral wagon in front of St. Patrick's Church, c. 1900

23

654-6 GRAND AVENUE

Marzullo's Pastry Shop *(former)*

Founded by Italian immigrant Giuseppe Marzullo in 1906, Marzullo's Pastry Shop used unwritten recipes Giuseppe learned as a youth in southern Italy and during his apprenticeship in New York prior to moving to New Haven. His sense of artistry and commitment to authentic recipes garnered international attention and won him awards locally as well as in Italy.

In the early years of the business, deliveries were made by bicycle and a borrowed horse-drawn carriage. Later, Giuseppe purchased a building at 163 Wallace Street, where the business acquired more modern equipment, refrigeration, and transportation. (His nephew, also named Giuseppe, and wife, Carmella, ran another Marzullo's Bakery on Washington Avenue, which opened during the Great Depression and lasted for nearly 40 years.) Marzullo's remained on Wallace Street for half a century.

By 1962, urban renewal plans forced the business to move. Giuseppe oversaw the construction of a new building at 656 Grand Avenue. After Giuseppe's death in 1967, his son Louis Marzullo and daughter Emilia Marzullo Esposito continued operating the bakery until 1987, when the iconic New Haven business closed.

Marzullo's reputation was such that people from all over Connecticut and even neighboring states would come in for their pastries, cookies, cakes, gelato, lemon ice, and holiday pies. The bakery's wedding cakes were particularly well-known and sought after. Every holiday, customers (some of them second- and third-generation customers) would wait in lines all the way around the building for their turn at the counter.

Some of the original cooking tools and a large copper kettle used in the bakery were donated by the Marzullo family to the Italian American Historical Society of Connecticut, whose archives are located at the Ethnic Heritage Center.

LEFT *163 Wallace Street Marzullo's c. 1950* TOP RIGHT *654 Grand Ave Marzullo's c 1970* BOTTOM RIGHT *Interior of 163 Wallace Street, l to r daughter Chiara Marzullo Tolli, Giuseppe Marzullo, wife Agata Marzullo, son Louis Marzullo, and daughter Emilia Marzullo Esposito*

24

137-9 WALLACE STREET

Lillian's Paradise *(demolished)*

Lillian Benford Lumpkin lived life on her own terms. She moved to New Haven from Opelika, Alabama, during the Great Migration with a dream of creating a new life as a financially independent businesswoman.

Lumpkin's career as an entrepreneur began on Dixwell Avenue, where African-Americans had created a bustling business community. There, she opened a successful soul food restaurant which tragically burned to the ground in the early 1950s. Her vision was never deterred, just expanded.

After purchasing a building on the corner of Wallace and Cain Streets, just off Grand Avenue, Lumpkin focused all of her energy on manifesting her long-held dream, Lillian's Paradise. She managed to borrow money for building renovations and to acquire a liquor license. Resourceful as ever, she found the support she needed and in October 1946 realized her dream. A newspaper announcement in the African-American press about the grand opening of Lillian's Paradise impatiently celebrated the launch "at last!" and invited patrons to visit the "finest restaurant and supper club in the East."

Lillian's Paradise featured fine food (including lobster and oysters), a wide selection of "choice wines," and top-notch entertainment. It seated 200 patrons,

and Lillian packed the club every weekend. Wild Man Steve was the master of ceremonies and Buck Halstead led a house orchestra. Lillian hosted banquets, church events, fraternal events, and other festivities. She personally drove to New York to review the finest entertainers and bring them to New Haven, where she often housed them overnight in apartments above the restaurant.

Jazz greats from Boston and New York found their way to Lillian's Paradise. Lillian's daughter, Shirley Lumpkin Gray, remembers performances by Lionel Hampton, Billie Holiday, Errol Garner, and Johnny Ray. Legendary pianist Horace Silver and jazz promoter George Wein both paid tribute to Lillian's Paradise in their memoirs.

In its heyday Lillian's Paradise was dubbed "Connecticut's Smartest Night Club" and listed in the *Green Book*, a road guide for African-American motorists that let people of color know the club was a safe place to visit, though it was also enjoyed by patrons of all races and nationalities.

Lillian Benford Lumpkin dreamed of seeing her name in lights. She achieved that goal long before her death at age 89.

LEFT *Lillian Benford Lumpkin* RIGHT *Live band at Lillian's Paradise*

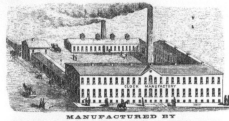

25

133 HAMILTON STREET

New Haven Clock Company *(partially demolished)*

The story of clock production in the area between downtown and the mouth of the Mill River touches on all aspects of New Haven's social, cultural, and economic history. Manufacturer Chauncey Jerome moved his clock company from Bristol to New Haven in 1884, settling on a two-acre site on the outskirts of Wooster Square. Jerome had begun his career apprenticing with renowned Connecticut clockmaker Eli Terry. Thanks to his discovery of a method of stamping rather than casting gears, Jerome was able to produce the lowest-priced clocks in the world at the time. He became wealthy as a manufacturer and leveraged his meteoric financial success into political influence, serving as a state legislator and mayor of New Haven.

Jerome's fortunes ran out in 1856 when he lost control of the clock company after a failed merger with a rival company controlled by circus impresario P.T. Barnum. Bankrupted and humiliated, Jerome left New Haven and died in poverty in 1868.

Jerome's original Greek Revival wood factory (located on the St. John Street side of the existing complex) burned down in 1866 and was immediately replaced with a larger neoclassical brick building that is the oldest wing of the factory still standing today.

The factory grew in an *ad hoc*, organic manner, with buildings being built and ex-

panded, or torn down and rebuilt, numerous times between 1866 and 1937. At its greatest extent, the factory was more than twice the size of the existing complex. It had 28 interconnected buildings on both sides of Hamilton Street, connected by a sky bridge. The complex was listed on the National Register of Historic Places in 2017.

In the early 1900s, the clock company flourished under the management of Walter Camp, who ran the factory while simultaneously coaching the football team at Yale College. During this period the company became one of the largest clockmakers in the world and the neighborhood's dominant employer, with as many as 2,000 workers turning out 500,000 timepieces every year. Its presence in the neighborhood drew immigrant workers from all over the world and supported a wide range of businesses centered on the commercial strip of Inner Grand Avenue. Factory workers and their families lived in tenement-style housing on the avenue as well as modest one- and two-family houses on side streets.

During World War I, the factory produced glow-in-the-dark watches with radium-laced dials for servicemen overseas. Some of the workers were young women who became known as "Radium Girls" because they experienced radiation poisoning or other health complications as a result of their work. During World War II, the company produced timing fuses and relays for mines, resuming clock production after the end of the war. Increasing foreign competition and slackening demand led to the factory's closure in 1956. Buildings on the west side of Hamilton Street were demolished in the 1960s to accommodate the construction of I-91.

After a period of abandonment, the clock factory complex enjoyed a second life in the 1980s and 1990s as inexpensively rented loft spaces that attracted raucous nightlife, punk rock venues, "adult" entertainment, motorcycle clubs, an indoor skate park, and counterculture activities of all kinds. In 2018 it was slated for redevelopment as residential lofts for artists but its fate is currently uncertain.

UPPER LEFT *New Haven Clock Company 1920 rendering* RIGHT *The women are boxing finished pocket watches while the young man in the foreground is doing some final assembling c. 1900* LOWER *1866 Rendering*

Acknowledgments

Some of the initial research for this book was done in the fall of 2019 by three seniors at Southern Connecticut State University majoring in journalism as part of their capstone project. Under the supervision of journalism professors Cindy Simoneau and Jodie Gil, students Faith Williams, Hunter O. Lyle, and Alfredo Rivera, Jr. visited the New Haven Museum and SCSU's Buley Library for information, conducted oral history interviews, and prepared an interactive map and videos. Their initial work helped us to raise the funding for the project from the Community Foundation of Greater New Haven and the Jewish Foundation of Greater New Haven. A Central Connecticut State University student intern, Kevin Skrocki, assisted with social media posts based on our research.

Other community members who have helped us include Joe Bartolino, President of SCSU, who has provided space to the EHC, continuing a tradition begun by President Michael Adanti in 1992; Jason Bischoff-Wurstle (Photo Archivist) and Margaret Anne Tockarshewsky (Executive Director) of the New Haven Museum; and local historians Bill Kraus, Colin M. Caplan and Joe Taylor, who shared their historic pictures and insights. Several former residents of the neighborhood who have inspired us with their stories, and guided tours include Alphonse Proto (author of *It was Grand! New Haven's St. Patrick's Church, Hamilton Street School and Memories of a Unique Neighborhood 1940-1966*, published in 2019), John Ragozzino, and Leo Marino. We extend a special thanks to Carole Bass for proofreading and editing the copy for this publication.

These are the members of each historical society who have participated in researching, writing and reviewing the entries which describe the cultural history of their community:

Jewish Historical Society of Greater New Haven: Rhoda Sachs Zahler Samuel (Project Coordinator), Aaron Goode (Research Coordinator and Editor), Marvin Bargar (JHS Archivist Emeritus), Patricia Illingworth (Research Archivist), Michael Dimenstein, Harold Miller, Robert Pierce Forbes, PhD., Judith Schiff (Chief Research Archivist of Sterling Memorial Library at Yale University)

Greater New Haven African American Historical Society: Co-Presidents Diane Petaway and Carolyn Baker, Edward Cherry, FAIA

Italian-American Historical Society of Connecticut: Laura Parisi, President

Connecticut Irish-American Historical Society: George Waldron, President, Patricia Heslin

Connecticut Ukrainian-American Historical Society: Gloria Horbaty, President, Donald Horbaty, Bohdan Sowa

Design and Publications Consultant: Jeanne Criscola, Criscola Design

Credits *(Note: all websites cited below were accessed October 31, 2021)*

PAGE 4 Map from Wooster Square Renewal Plan, 1965.

PAGES 6-12 Text sources: Ladin, Harvey. "The Grand Avenue Jews." *Jews in New Haven, Volume II*, Jewish Historical Society of Greater New Haven, 1979 pp. 84-97; Stein, Peter. "A Truly Grand Avenue." Paper for Yale University course, 1998; Miller, Harold; Proto, Al; Raggozino, John. Oral history interviews conducted by Southern CT State University Journalism students, 2019; Connecticut Irish-American Historical Society. *The Shanachie*, Volume 25, Number 1, 2013. DigitalCommons@SHU. https://digitalcommons.sacredheart.edu/shanachie/37/; Osterweis, Rollin G. *Three Centuries of New Haven, 1638-1938*, New Haven: Yale University Press, 1953; Ancestry. com; U.S. Census and City Directory Data; Caplan, Colin M. *A Guide to Historic New Haven Connecticut*, The History Press, 2007; Taylor, William. Taylor's Legislative History and Souvenir of Connecticut, Vol. V, 1905-1906; O'Donnell, Rev. James H. "History of the Diocese of Hartford."; The Ethnic History of New Haven, a poster project of the Ethnic Heritage Center; Rae, Douglas, *City: Urbanism and Its End*, Yale University Press, 2003; Townshend, Doris. *The Streets of New Haven: The Origins of their Names*, New Haven Colony Historical Society, 1998.

PAGE 6 Maps courtesy of https://newhavenurbanism.wordpress.com/new-haven-history/paradise-lost/, side by side picture of maps courtesy of Jonathan Hopkins.

PAGE 8 Photo courtesy of New Haven Museum.

PAGES 9 AND 12 Photos courtesy of Jewish Historical Society of Greater New Haven.

PAGE 11 Photo courtesy of Colin M. Caplan.

PAGE 16 Photo courtesy of Jewish Historical Society of Greater New Haven. Text source: Michael Dimenstein, President, Congregation Mishkan Israel, Information prepared for CMI Anniversary Celebration; Osterweis, Rollin G. "Mishkan Israel 1840-1960," The Papers of Congregation Mishkan Israel. http://www.newhavenmuseum.org/wp-content/uploads/2013/06/MSS-B54.pdf; *Jews in New Haven*, Vol. II, Jewish Historical Society, 1979, pp. 104-108.

PAGE 17 Photos courtesy of the *New Haven Independent* and Aaron Goode. Text source: Rafael A. Melendez obituary. Legacy.com, *New Haven Register*, July 20-21, 2015, https://www.legacy.com/obituaries/nhregister/obituary.aspx?n=rafael-a-melendez&pid=175327287&fhid=4177; Czepiel, Kathy Leonard. "Joint Venture," *Daily Nutmeg*, January 7, 2020, http://dailynutmeg.com/2020/01/07/junta-progressive-action-joint-venture/; Rierden, Andi. "Puerto Ricans Are Facing Setbacks in New Haven." *New York Times*. February 16, 1992, Section CN, Page 12, https://www.nytimes.com/1992/02/16/nyregion/problems-temper-puerto-ricans-success.html; Sanders, Alexandra. "Pioneer of New Haven's Latino community, Rafael Melendez Sr., honored with city street corner sign." *New Haven Register*. October 1, 2012, https://www.nhregister.com/news/article/Pioneer-of-New-Haven-s-Latino-community-Rafael-11547957.php.

PAGES 18-19 Copies of school records from Annual Report of the Board of Education of the New Haven City School District, 1861; Picture courtesy of Yale University Library, map from Warner, Robert Austin, *New Haven Negroes: A Social History*, New Haven: Yale University Press, 1940. Text Sources: Feinberg, Harvey J. "Black New Haven Residents During the Nineteenth Century: Resources Located in the Whitney Library, New Haven Museum and Historical Society," Connecticut History Review, Vol. 57, No. 2 (Fall 2018), pp. 197-212; Marcin, Raymond B. "Nineteenth Century De Jure School Segregation in Connecticut," Connecticut Bar Journal, Vol. 45, Issue 3, 1971, pp. 394-400; Annual Report of the Board of Education of the New Haven City School District," various years 1850-1868, accessed at https://bit.ly/3EbclbH; Piascik, Andy, "Edward Alexander Bouchet: The First African-American to Earn a PhD from an American University," ConnecticutHistory.org, February 12, 2020, https://connecticuthistory.org/edward-alexander-bouchet-the-first-african-american-to-earn-a-phd-from-an-american-university/.

PAGE 20 Photos courtesy of DelMonico's website. Text sources: DelMonico Hatter website, https://www.delmonicohatter.com/; Torrellas, Derek. "DelMonico's 4th Generation Hats a City." *New Haven Independent*, March 24, 2015, https://www.newhavenindependent.org/index.php/archives/entry/four_generations_of_hatters_in_new_haven/.

PAGE 21 Photos courtesy of Peter Faggio. Text sources: Interview with Peter Faggio conducted by Rhoda Zahler Samuel; Lucibello, Mary and Barbieri, Norma, "The Story of Frank Lucibello." *La Storia*, publication of the Italian-American Historical Society of Connecticut, Volume 13, Number 4, 2004.

PAGE 22 Photos courtesy of Aaron Goode, Robert Unger. Text sources: Interview with Robert Unger conducted by Rhoda Zahler Samuel.

PAGE 23 Photos courtesy of the Jewish Historical Society of Greater New Haven. Text sources: Ladin, Harvey. "The Grand Avenue Jews." *Jews in New Haven, Volume II*. Edited by Dr. Barry Herman, Jewish Historical Society of Greater New Haven, October 1979, pp. 84-97.

PAGE 24 Photo courtesy of Joe Taylor. Text sources: "The Grand Avenue Jews," *Jews in New Haven, Volume II, ibid.*

PAGE 25 Photos courtesy of Grace Z. Marriott. Text sources: Family history from Grace Z. Marriott; Falcigno, Paul A., *The Tapestry of Life, A Eulogy of Mother, Archives of the Italian-American Historical Society of Connecticut*, March, 1995.

PAGE 26 Photos courtesy of Colin M. Caplan and Anthony Riccio. Text sources: Cinema Treasures Website http://cinematreasures.org/theaters/19145; Drake, James, , Amadeus Press, 1997; Riccio, Anthony. *The Italian American Experience in New Haven: Images and Oral Histories*, SUNY Press, 2006; Cannelli, Antonio, *La Colonia Italiana di New Haven, Connecticut,* (Stabilimento Tipgrafico A. Cannelli Co.), 1921.

PAGE 27 Photos courtesy of Aaron Goode and Artie Shaw: https://picryl.com/media/artie-shaw-playing-857292 and https://swingandbeyond.com/2020/09/19/any-old-time-1938-artie-shaw-and-billie-holiday/. Text sources: New Haven Building Archive, https://nhba.yale.edu/; Shaw, Artie, *The Trouble with Cinderella: An Outline of Identity*, Farrar, Straus and Young, 1952.

PAGE 28 Photos courtesy of the *New Haven Independent* and Aaron Goode (site photo). Text source: Appel, Allan. "Memorial Day, Lenzi Park, New Haven." *New Haven Independent*, May 29, 2007, https://www.newhavenindependent.org/index.php/archives/entry/memorial_day_lenzi_park_new_haven/.

PAGE 29 Photos courtesy of Jewish Historical Society of Greater New Haven page 30 Library of Congress, Lewis Hine photo for the National Child Labor Committee. Text sources: Interviews with Frank Carrano, John Ragozzino, Alphonse Proto conducted by Rhoda Zahler Samuel and SCSU Journalism students; Proto, Alphonse. *It Was Grand! New Haven's St. Patrick's Church, Hamilton Street School and Memories of a Unique Neighborhood 1940-1966*, Foz llc, 2019.

PAGE 31 Photo courtesy of the Jewish Historical Society of Greater New Haven. Text sources: Ladin, Harvey. "The Grand Avenue Jews." *Jews in New Haven Volume II,* Jewish Historical Society of Greater New Haven, 1979, pp. 84-98; *Jews in New Haven, Volume VI*, edited by Werner S. Hirsch, Jewish Historical of New Haven, 1993, p. 181.

PAGE 32 Photos courtesy of Harold Miller. Text sources: Zahler, Rhoda Sachs, Video interviews with Harold Miller, Jewish Historical Society of Greater New Haven Video Archives; Zahler, Rhoda Sachs, "Interview with Harold Miller", *Jews in New Haven, Volume IX*, Edited by David S. Fischer, M.D., Jewish Historical Society of Greater New Haven, 2009, pp. 302-309; Williams, Faith, Lyle, Hunter, Rivera, Alfredo, Southern Connecticut State University journalism capstone project interview and video, 2019-20.

PAGE 33 Photos courtesy of Aaron Goode (building), and Taylor, William. *Taylor's Legislative History and Souvenir of Connecticut Vol VI 1907-1908*, p, 22. Text sources: Caplan, Colin. *A Guide* to *Historic New Haven, Connecticut*. Arcadia Publishing, 2006; Taylor, William, ibid.; U.S. Census Data; New Haven City Directories.

PAGE 34 Photos courtesy of the *New Haven Register*, and the Lender Family. Text sources: Horowitz, Andy, "The Lender Family of New Haven", *Jews in New Haven, Vol. IX*, Edited by David S. Fischer, M.D., pp. 191-219; Turmelle, Luther, "Lender's factory History," *New Haven Register*, March 1, 2000; Caplan, Colin M., *Lender's Bagel History*, a Zoom presentation for the Jewish Historical Society of Greater New Haven, March 7, 2021; Interview with Marvin Lender conducted by Rhoda Zahler Samuel.

PAGE 35 Photos courtesy of George Scali (interior) and Joe Taylor (exterior). Text sources: O'Donnell, Rev. James H. History of the Diocese of Hartford; Proto, Alphonse, *It Was Grand! New Haven's St. Patrick's Church, Hamilton Street School and Memories of a Unique Neighborhood 1940-1966*, Foz LLC, 2019; *The Shanachie* Vol. XXV, No. 1, 2013, https://digitalcommons.sacredheart.edu/cgi/viewcontent.cgi?article=1039&context=shanachie.

PAGE 36-37 Photos courtesy of Elm City Communities archives. Text sources: Rae, Douglas. *City: Urbanism and Its End*, Yale University Press, 2003; http://digital.janeaddams.ramapo.edu/items/show/4043; Archives and Annual Reports of Housing Authority of New Haven (now Elm City Communities).

PAGE 38 Photos courtesy of the Jewish Historical Society of Greater New Haven (building) and Scott Rosner (family). Text sources: Interview with Scott Rosner conducted by Rhoda Zahler Samuel; New Haven Building Archive, https://nhba.yale.edu/; Proto, Alphonse, *It Was Grand! New Haven's St. Patrick's Church, Hamilton Street School and Memories of a Unique Neighborhood 1940-1966*. Foz LLC, 2019, p.74.

PAGE 39 Photos courtesy of Victoria Ferraro. Text sources: https://nhba.yale.edu/building?id=58e6b948adb817121752a693; "Ferraro's Market - New Haven, CT - About Us." Ferraromarket.com, 2020, www.ferraromarket.com/about-us. Accessed 13 Jan. 2020; *New Haven Register*; https://www.ctinsider.com/news/nhregister/article/Ferarro-s-to-close-longtime-New-Haven-store-on-15815169.php; https://www.nhregister.com/news/article/Meat-King-Farms-looks-to-make-its-mark-on-New-15834707.php; New Haven Independent articles; https://www.newhavenindependent.org/index.php/archives/entry/deal_near_on_ferraros_replacement/; https://www.newhavenindependent.org/index.php/archives/entry/ferraros_north_haven/; Phone interviews with Victoria Ferraro conducted by Rhoda Zahler Samuel, 2020.

PAGE 40 Photo courtesy of Carmine Monaco from Sisk Bros. Text sources: U.S. Census Data; New Haven City Directories; "History & Staff," Sisk Brothers Funeral Home, www.siskbrothers.com/who-we-are/history-and-staff.

PAGE 41 Photos courtesy of the New Haven Museum and the Marzullo/Esposito family. Text sources: Proto, Alphonse, *It Was Grand!*, Foz LLC, 2019; "The Fine Art of Baking; It takes More Than Just Dough," *The Register Magazine*, September 23, 1962, p.3; The Marzullo/Esposito Family documents.

PAGES 42-43 Photos courtesy of Mrs. Shirley Lumpkin Gray and the collection of Lucille Mapp (by way of Frank Mitchell). Text sources: Interview with Mrs. Shirley Lumpkin Gray by Carolyn Baker; "Monterey Memories," *New Haven Independent*, 2 Feb. 2018, https://www.newhavenindependent.org/index.php/archives/entry/conncat_swings_jazz_past/; Unsung Heroes: The Music of Jazz in New Haven, Rebecca Abbott, W. Frank Mitchell. 2001. (video)https://vimeo.com/387143627.

PAGES 44-45 Photo courtesy of Bill Kraus, page 45 photo courtesy of the New Haven Museum. Text sources: *Carriages and Clocks, Corsets and Locks: The Rise and Fall of an Industrial City—New Haven, Connecticut*, Edited by Preston Maynard and Marjorie B. Noyes, Hanover, N.H, University Press of New England, 2004, pp. 171-176; http://www.nationalclockrepair.com/Jerome_Clock_History.php; Interviews with Bill Kraus by SCSU Journalism students and Rhoda Zahler Samuel, 2019-2021.

SPONSORS

PLATINUM SPONSORS | $2,000 – $5,000
Community Foundation of Greater New Haven

GOLD SPONSORS | $500 – $1,999
Connecticut Irish American Historical Society
Jewish Federation/Foundation of Greater New Haven
Jewish Historical Society of Greater New Haven
Laura and Robert Parisi

SILVER SPONSORS | $200 - $499
Connecticut Ukrainian American Historical Society
Greater New Haven African American Historical Society
St. Patrick's Alumni
Harold Miller
Rhoda Sachs-Zahler Samuel

FRIENDS | $20 – $199
Donald and Gloria Horbaty
Grace Z. Marriott
Diane Petaway
Bohdan Sowa